EASY GUITAR
WITH NOTES & TAB

Guitar Instrumentals

T0048158

ISBN 0-634-04855-4

HAL•LEONARD®
CORPORATION

7777 W. BLUEMOUND RD. P.O. BOX 13819 MILWAUKEE, WI 53213

Visit Hal Leonard Online at
www.halleonard.com

Guitar Instrumentals

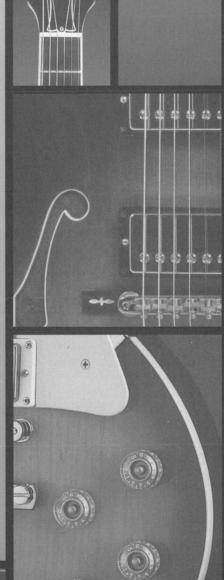

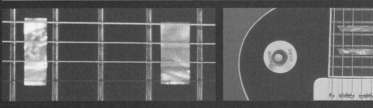

Guitar Notation Legend

Guitar Music can be notated three different ways: on a *musical staff*, in *tablature*, and in *rhythm slashes*.

RHYTHM SLASHES are written above the staff. Strum chords in the rhythm indicated. Use the chord diagrams found at the top of the first page of the transcription for the appropriate chord voicings. Round noteheads indicate single notes.

THE MUSICAL STAFF shows pitches and rhythms and is divided by bar lines into measures. Pitches are named after the first seven letters of the alphabet.

TABLATURE graphically represents the guitar fingerboard. Each horizontal line represents a string, and each number represents a fret.

4th string, 2nd fret   1st & 2nd strings open, open D chord played together

HALF-STEP BEND: Strike the note and bend up 1/2 step.

WHOLE-STEP BEND: Strike the note and bend up one step.

GRACE NOTE BEND: Strike the note and immediately bend up as indicated.

SLIGHT (MICROTONE) BEND: Strike the note and bend up 1/4 step.

BEND AND RELEASE: Strike the note and bend up as indicated, then release back to the original note. Only the first note is struck.

PRE-BEND: Bend the note as indicated, then strike it.

VIBRATO: The string is vibrated by rapidly bending and releasing the note with the fretting hand.

WIDE VIBRATO: The pitch is varied to a greater degree by vibrating with the fretting hand.

HAMMER-ON: Strike the first (lower) note with one finger, then sound the higher note (on the same string) with another finger by fretting it without picking.

PULL-OFF: Place both fingers on the notes to be sounded. Strike the first note and without picking, pull the finger off to sound the second (lower) note.

LEGATO SLIDE: Strike the first note and then slide the same fret-hand finger up or down to the second note. The second note is not struck.

SHIFT SLIDE: Same as legato slide, except the second note is struck.

TRILL: Very rapidly alternate between the notes indicated by continuously hammering on and pulling off.

TAPPING: Hammer ("tap") the fret indicated with the pick-hand index or middle finger and pull off to the note fretted by the fret hand.

NATURAL HARMONIC: Strike the note while the fret-hand lightly touches the string directly over the fret indicated.

Harm.

PINCH HARMONIC: The note is fretted normally and a harmonic is produced by adding the edge of the thumb or the tip of the index finger of the pick hand to the normal pick attack.

P.H.

PICK SCRAPE: The edge of the pick is rubbed down (or up) the string, producing a scratchy sound.

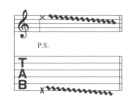

P.S.

MUFFLED STRINGS: A percussive sound is produced by laying the fret hand across the string(s) without depressing, and striking them with the pick hand.

PALM MUTING: The note is partially muted by the pick hand lightly touching the string(s) just before the bridge.

P.M.

RAKE: Drag the pick across the strings indicated with a single motion.

rake

TREMOLO PICKING: The note is picked as rapidly and continuously as possible.

VIBRATO BAR DIVE AND RETURN: The pitch of the note or chord is dropped a specified number of steps (in rhythm) then returned to the original pitch.

w/ bar

VIBRATO BAR SCOOP: Depress the bar just before striking the note, then quickly release the bar.

w/ bar

VIBRATO BAR DIP: Strike the note and then immediately drop a specified number of steps, then release back to the original pitch.

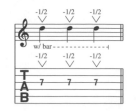

w/ bar

STRUM AND PICK PATTERNS

This chart contains the suggested strum and pick patterns that are referred to by number at the beginning of each song in this book. The symbols ⊓ and ∨ in the strum patterns refer to down and up strokes, respectively. The letters in the pick patterns indicate which right-hand fingers plays which strings.

p = thumb
i = index finger
m = middle finger
a = ring finger

For example; Pick Pattern 2
is played: thumb - index - middle - ring

You can use the 3/4 Strum or Pick Patterns in songs written in compound meter (6/8, 9/8, 12/8, etc.).
For example, you can accompany a song in 6/8 by playing the 3/4 pattern twice in each measure.
The 4/4 Strum and Pick Patterns can be used for songs written in cut time (¢) by doubling the note time values in the patterns. Each pattern would therefore last two measures in cut time.

The Claw

By Jerry Reed

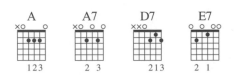

Strum Pattern: 3
Pick Pattern: 4

Fast Country Rock

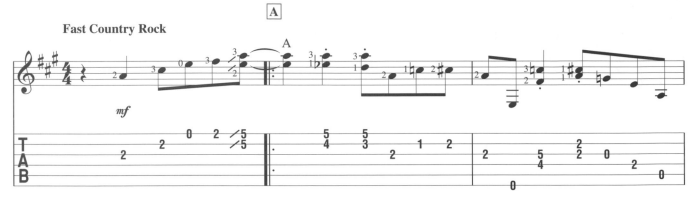

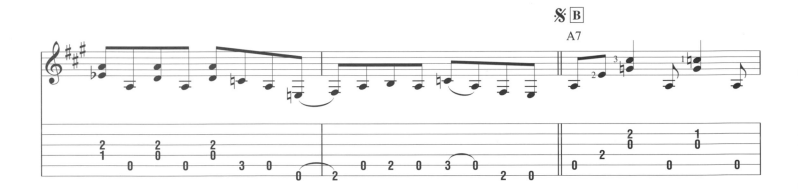

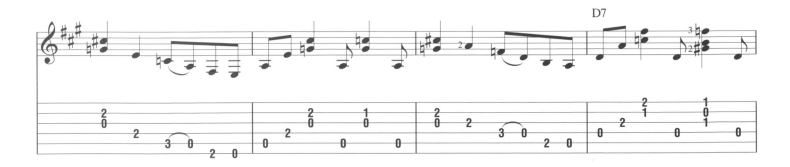

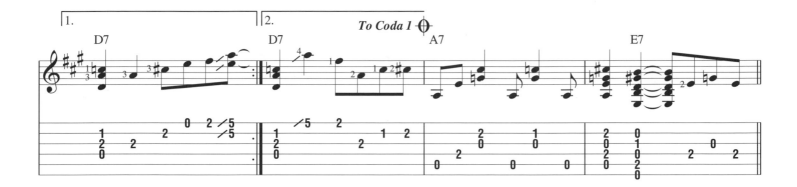

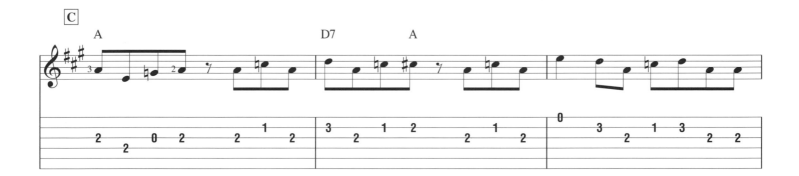

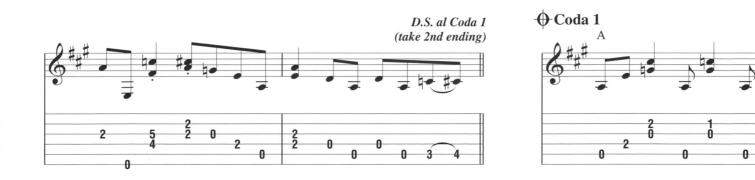

D.S. al Coda 2
(take 1st ending)

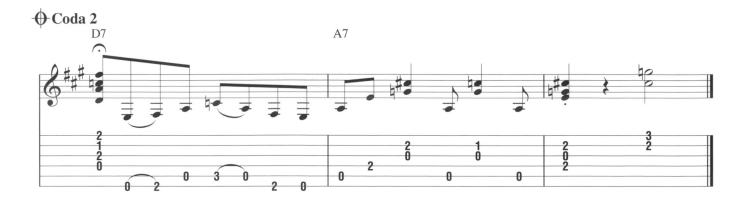

Forty Miles of Bad Road

By Duane Eddy and Al Casey

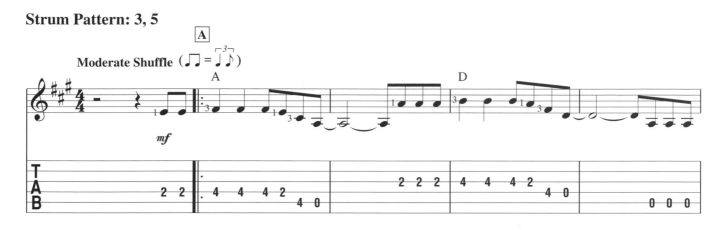

Strum Pattern: 3, 5

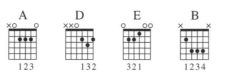

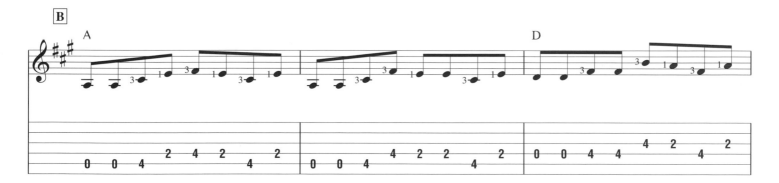

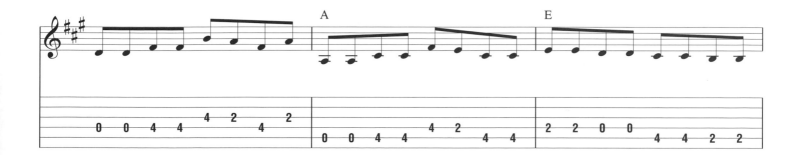

9

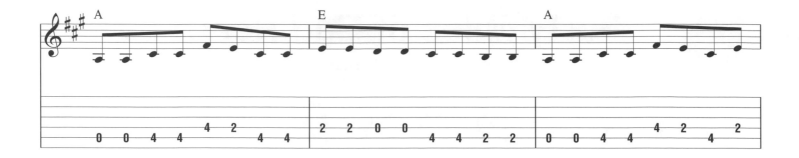

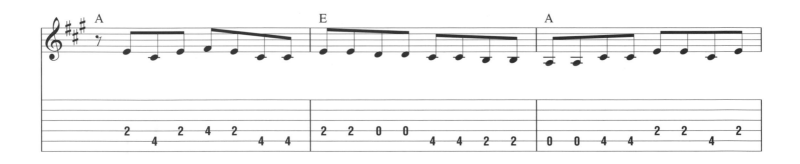

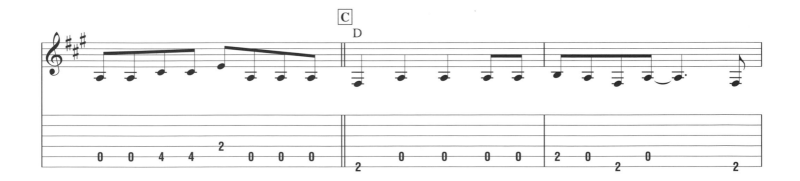

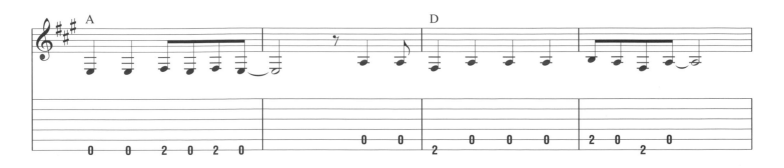

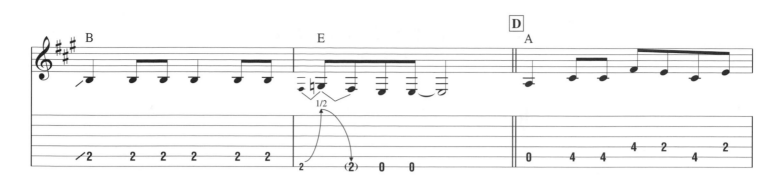

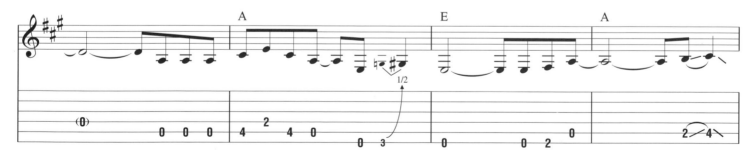

Frankenstein

By Edgar Winter

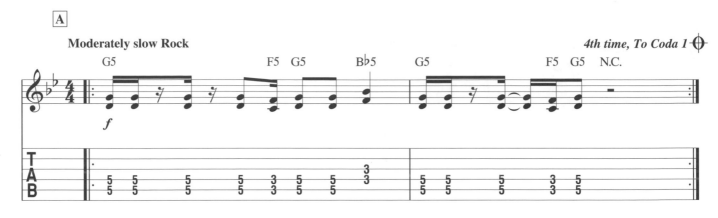

Strum Pattern: 1

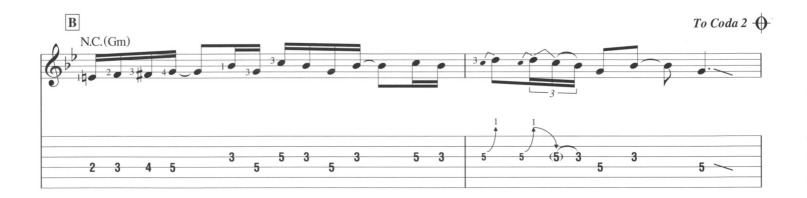

2nd time, D.C. al Coda 1
(take repeat)

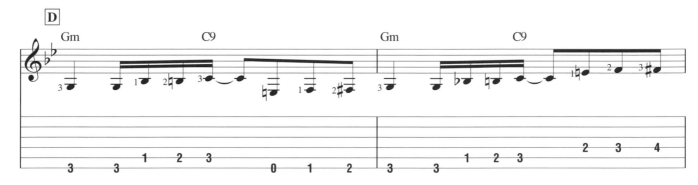

⊕ Coda 1

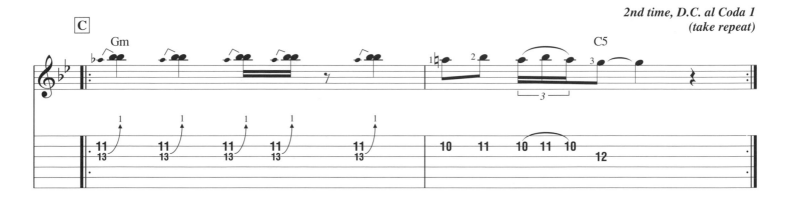

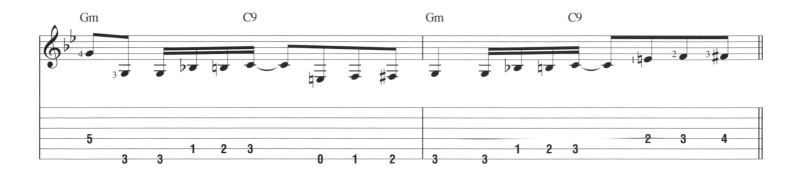

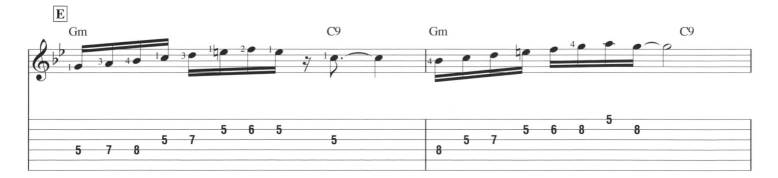

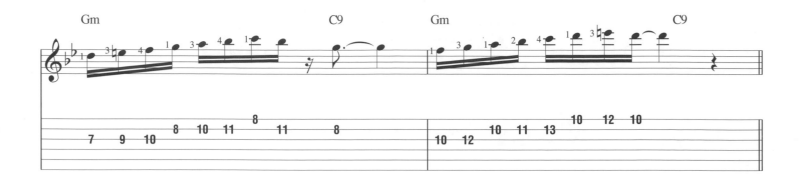

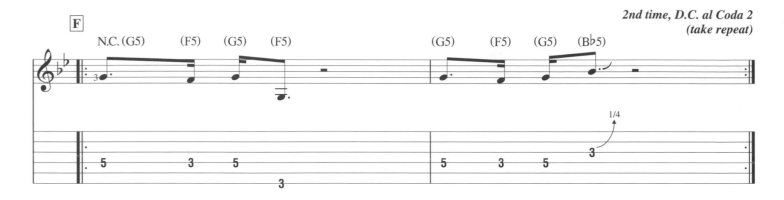

2nd time, D.C. al Coda 2
(take repeat)

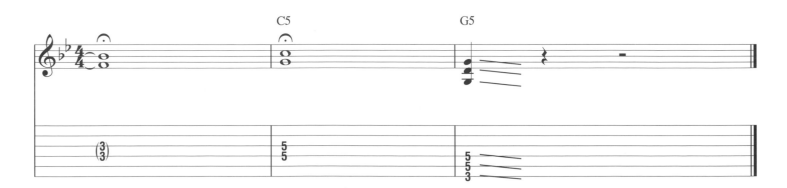

Freeway Jam

By Max Middleton

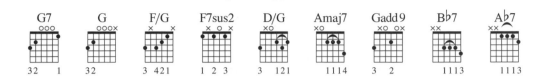

Strum Pattern: 2
Pick Pattern: 4

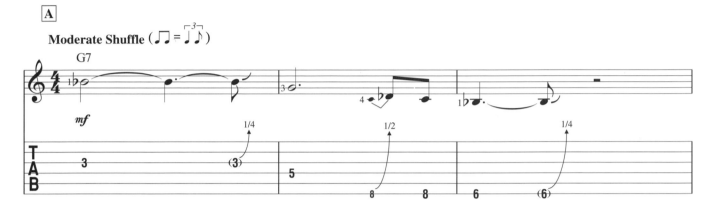

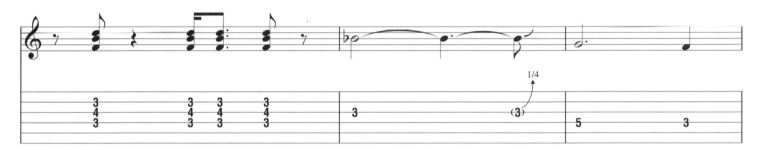

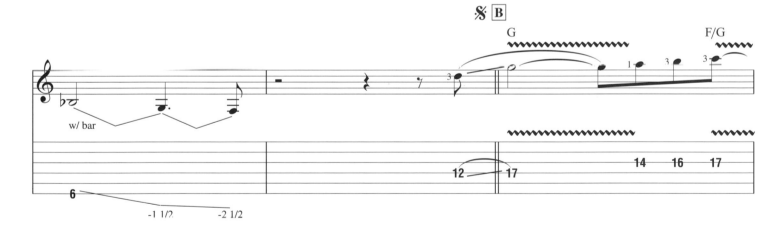

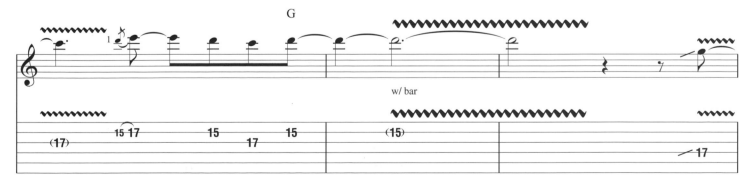

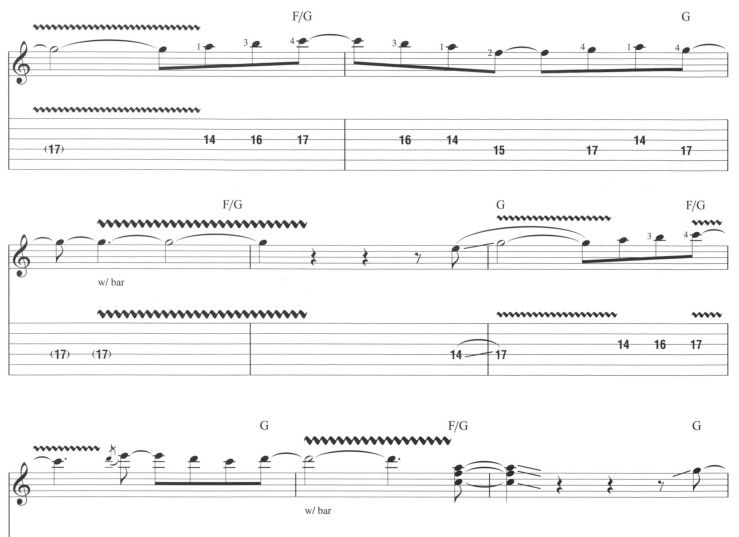

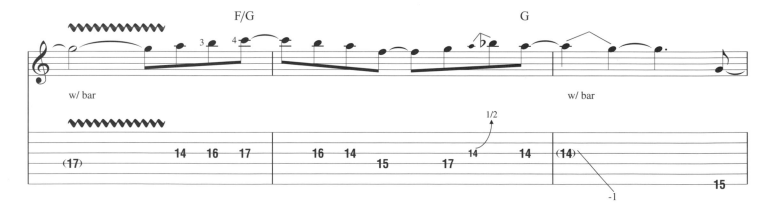

2nd time, Fade out

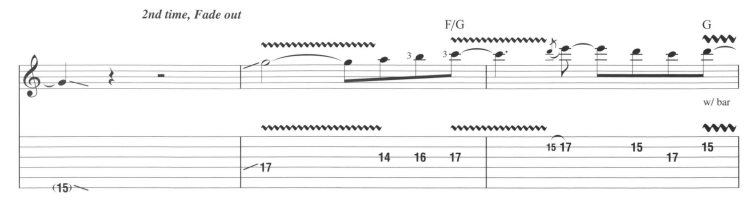

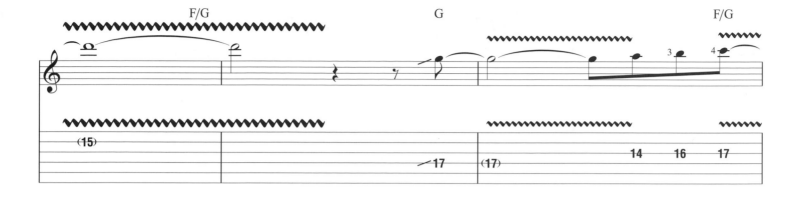

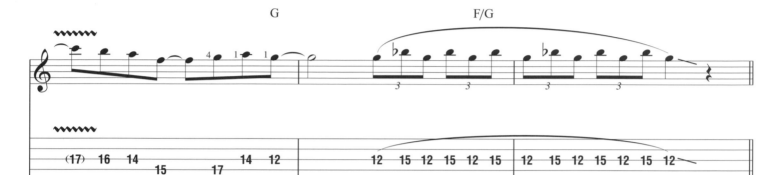

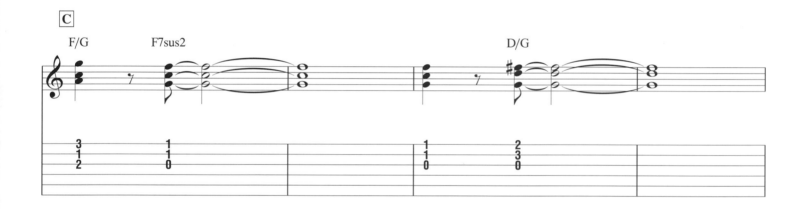

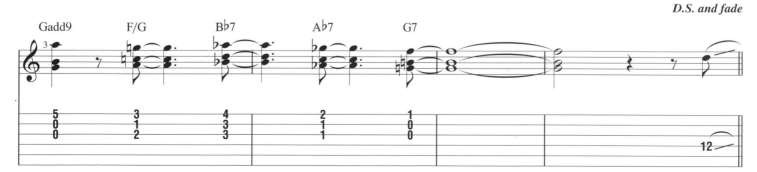

Green Onions

Written by Al Jackson, Jr., Lewis Steinberg, Booker T. Jones and Steve Cropper

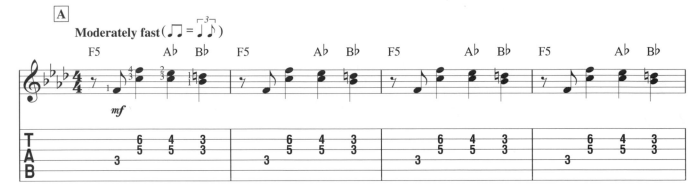

Strum Pattern: 4

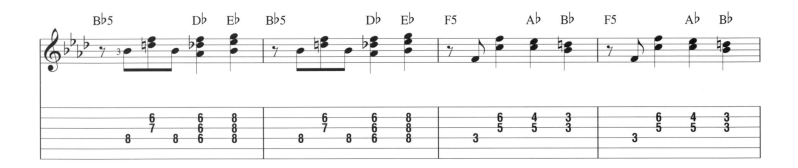

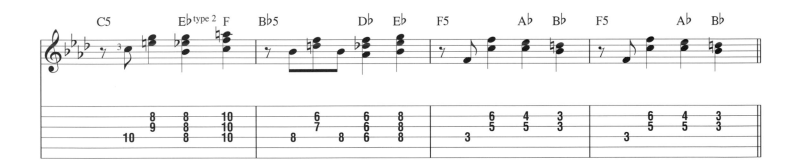

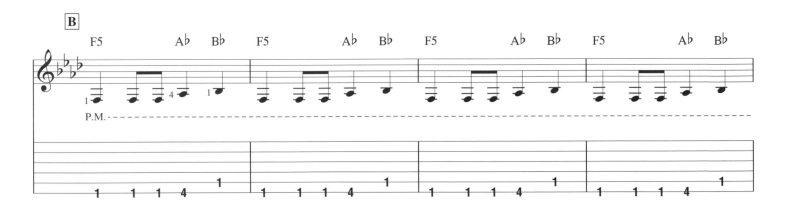

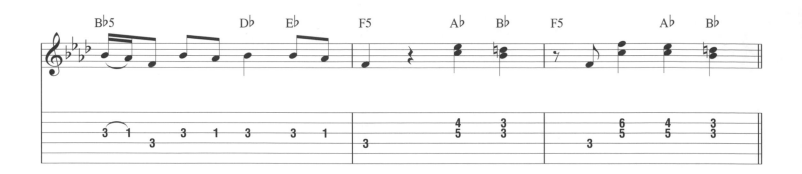

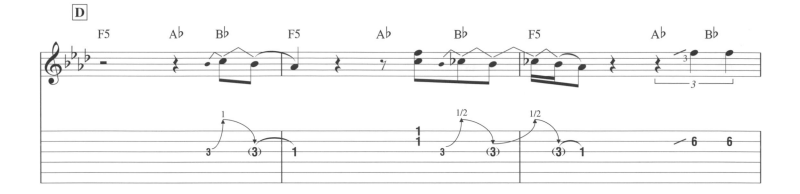

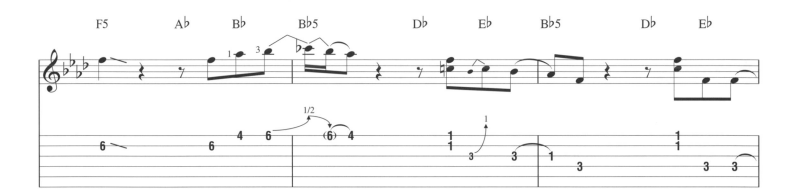

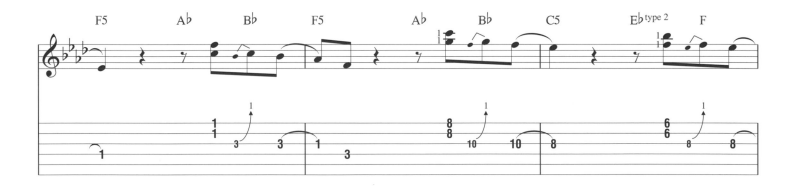

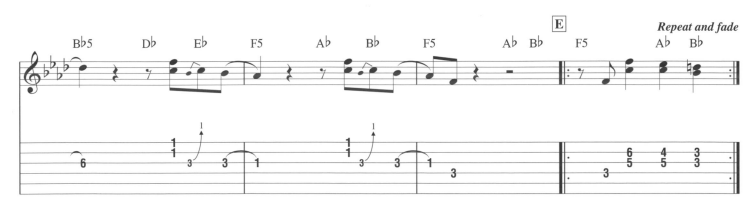

Rebel 'Rouser

By Duane Eddy and Lee Hazlewood

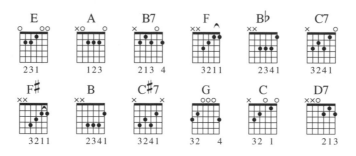

Strum Pattern: 4
Pick Pattern: 3

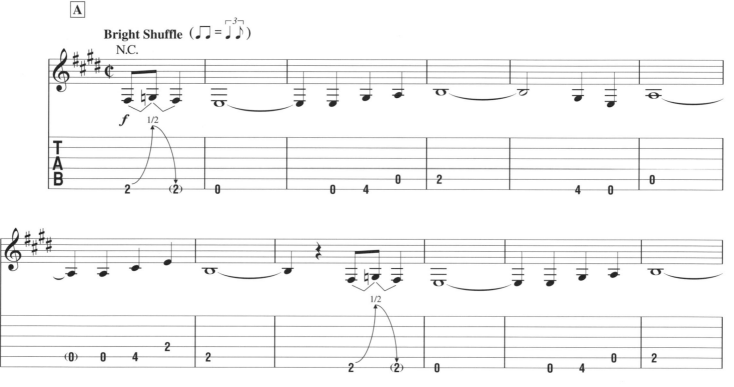

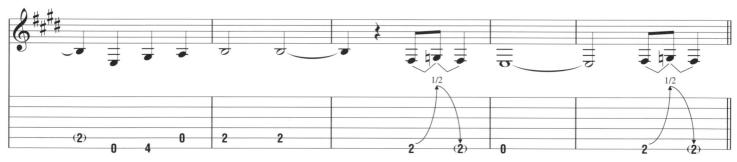

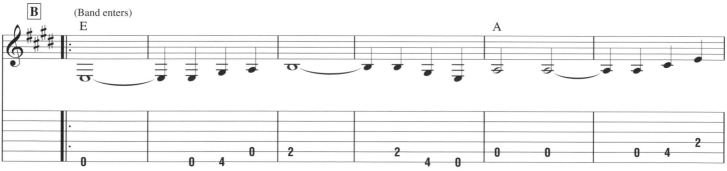

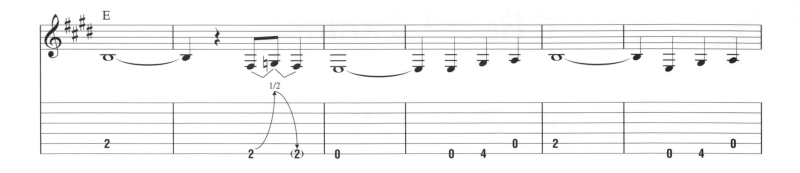

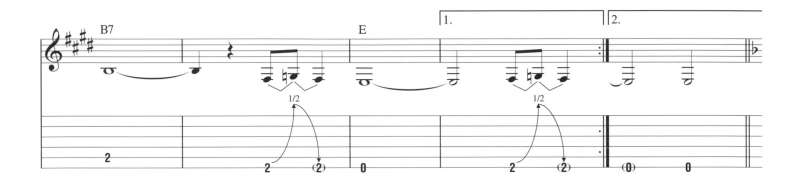

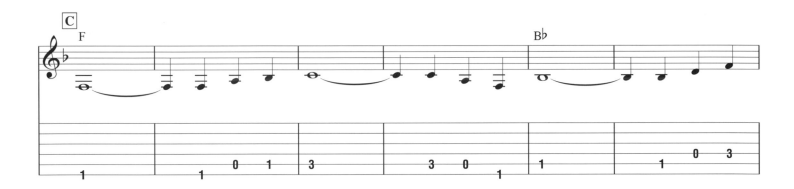

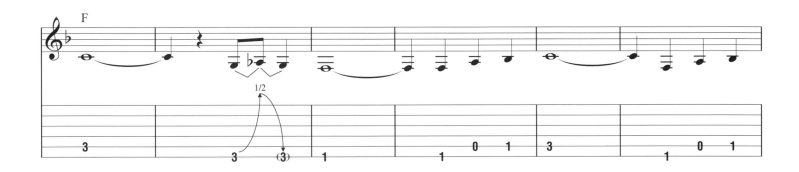

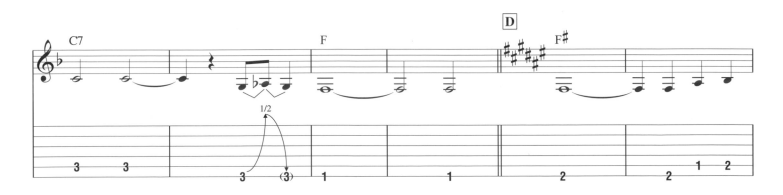

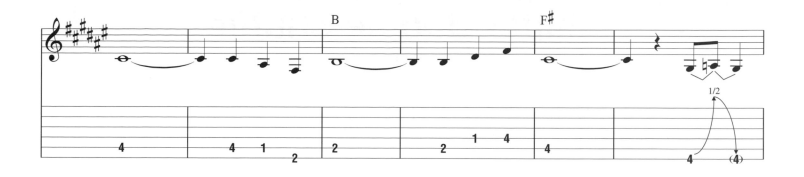

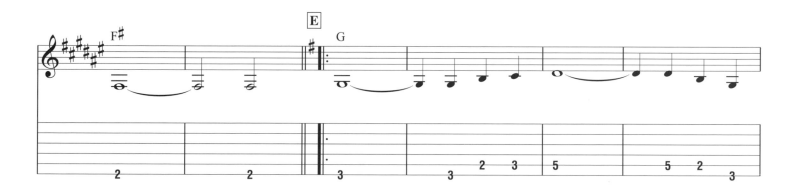

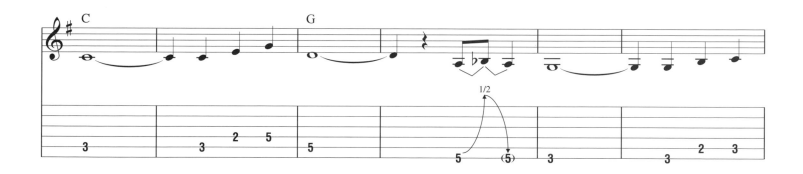

Repeat and fade

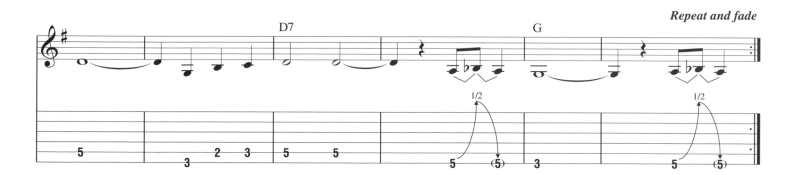

Guitar Boogie Shuffle

By Arthur Smith

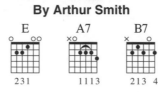

Strum Pattern: 3, 4
Pick Pattern: 3, 4

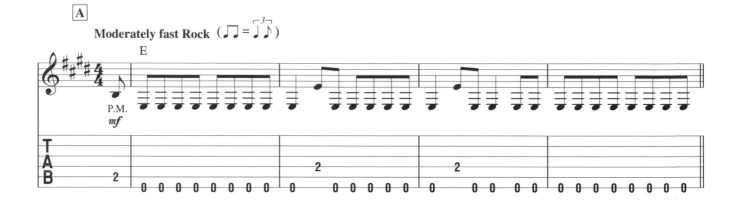

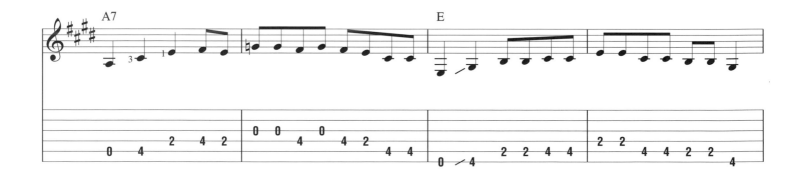

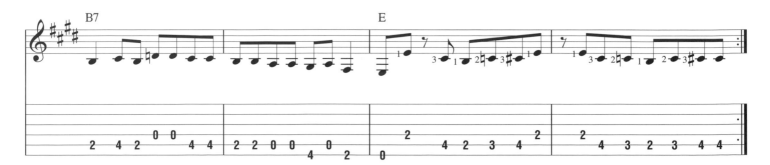

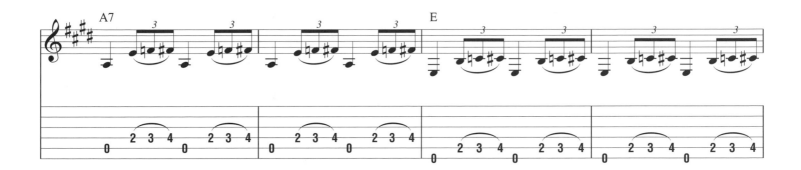

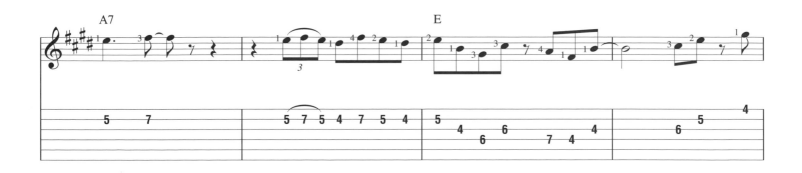

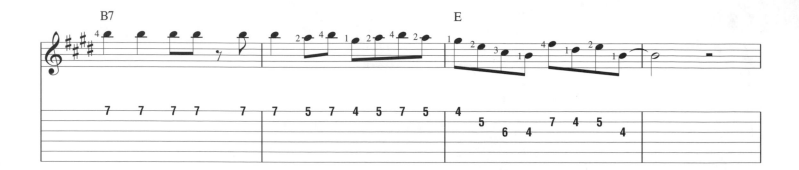

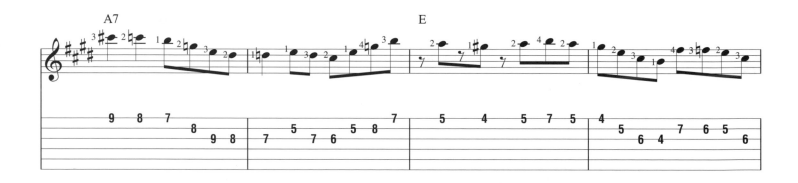

D.S. al Coda

Coda

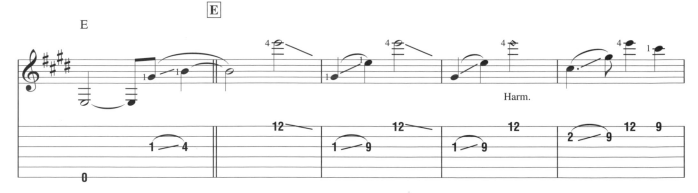

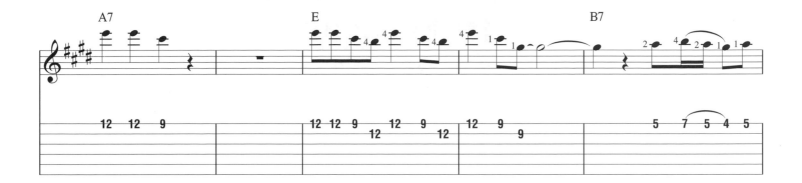

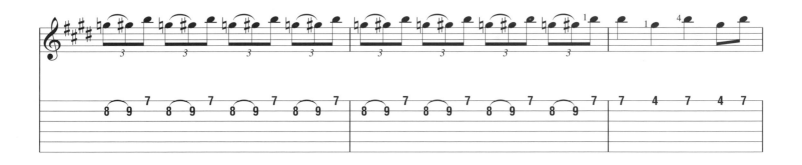

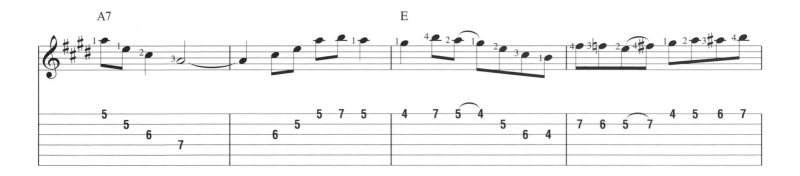

D.S.S. and fade
(take repeat)

Hide Away

By Freddie King and Sonny Thompson

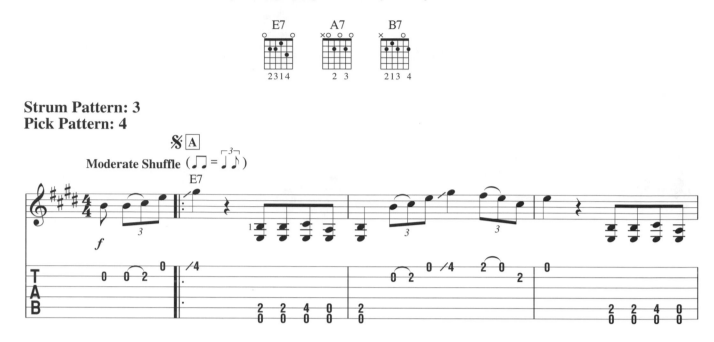

Strum Pattern: 3
Pick Pattern: 4

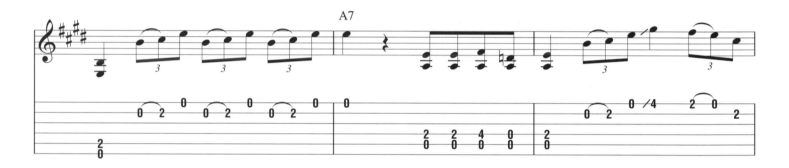

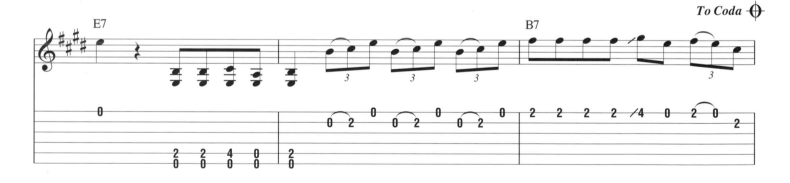

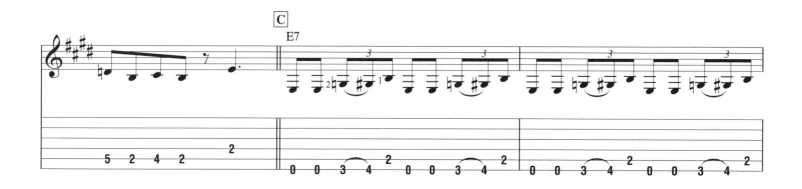

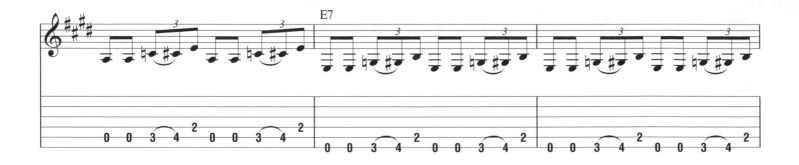

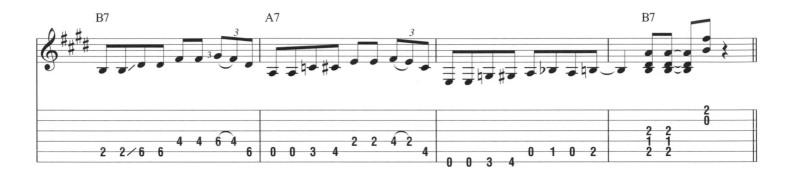

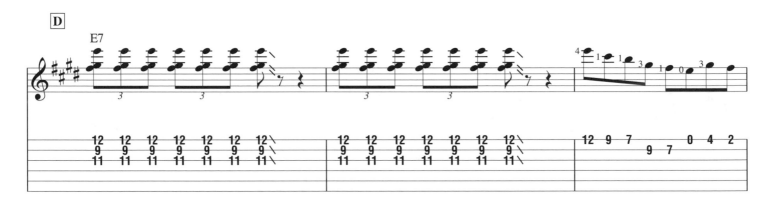

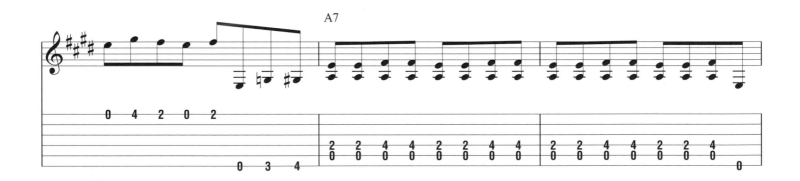

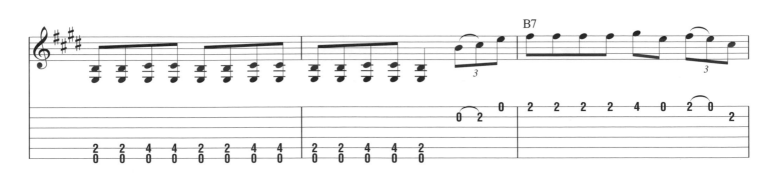

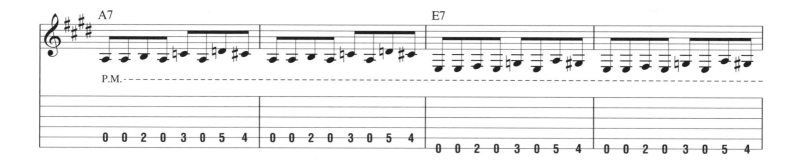

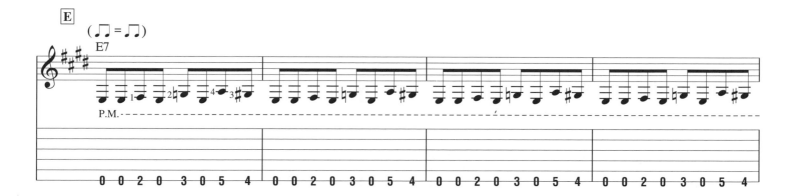

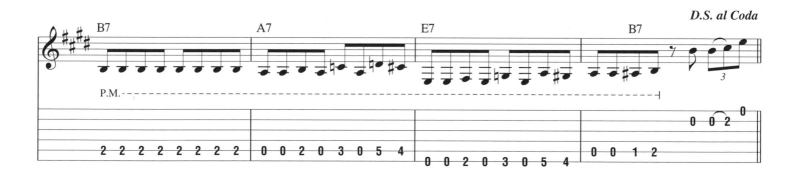

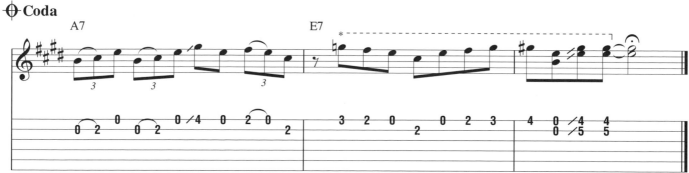

*Played as even eighth notes.

Jessica

Written by Dickey Betts

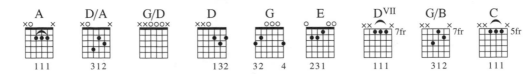

Strum Pattern: 3, 4
Pick Pattern: 3, 4

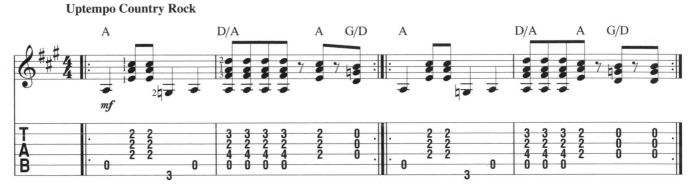

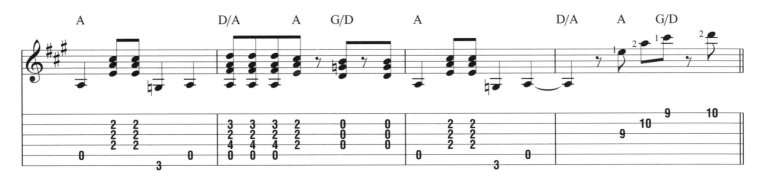

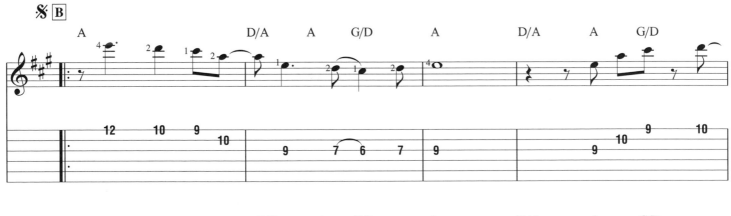

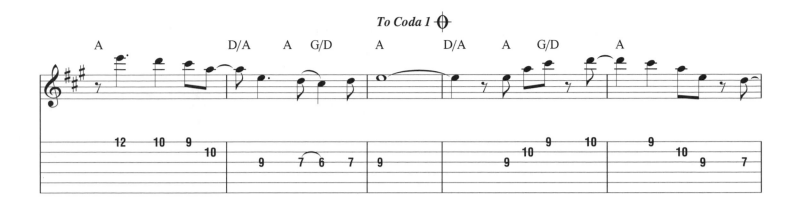

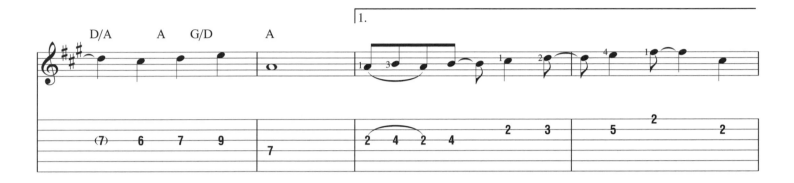

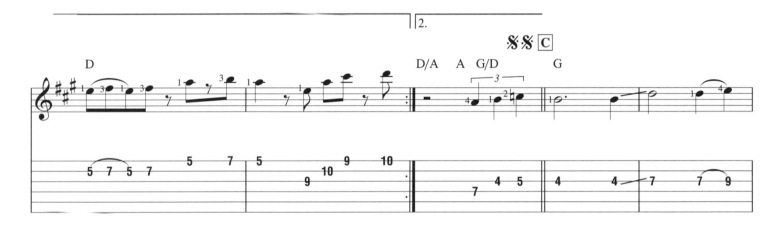

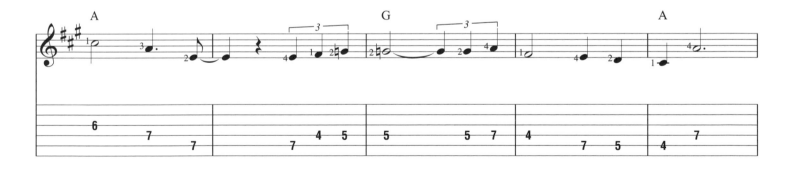

1st time, D.S. al Coda 1

2nd time, To Coda 2

Coda 1

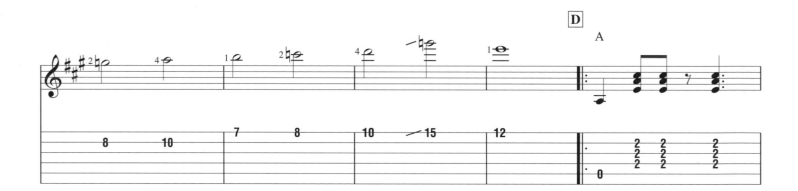

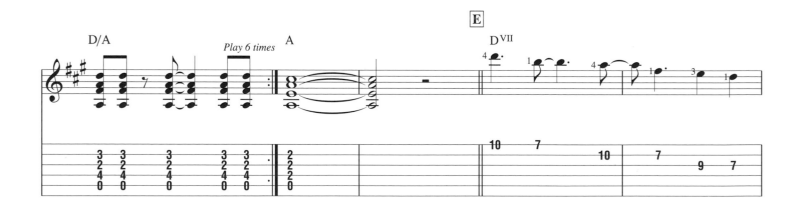

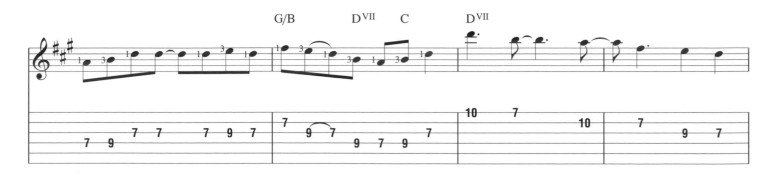

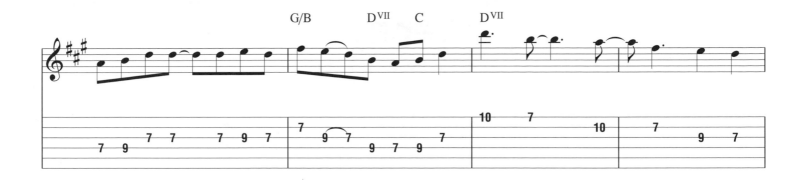

⊕ Coda 2

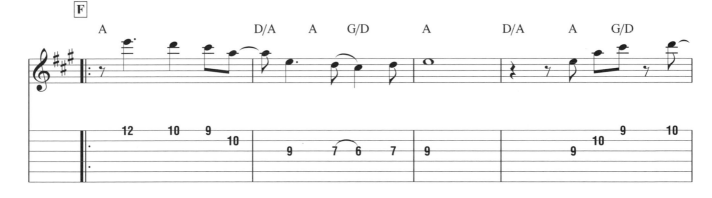

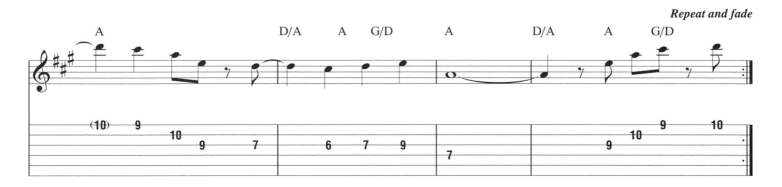

Lenny

Written by Stevie Ray Vaughan

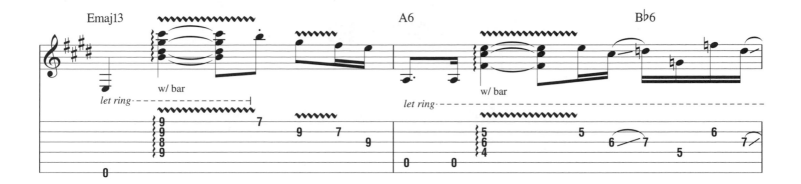

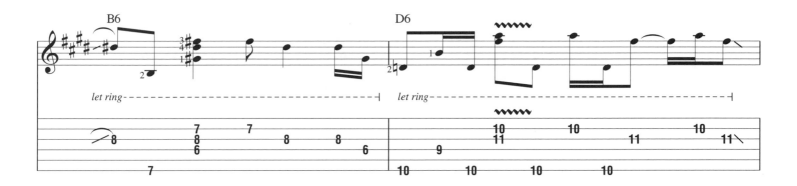

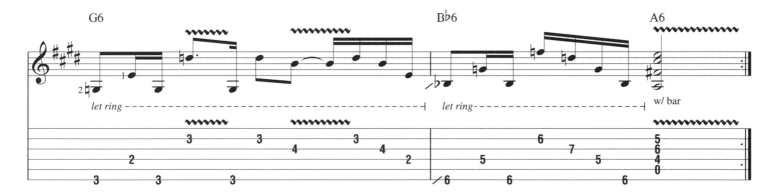

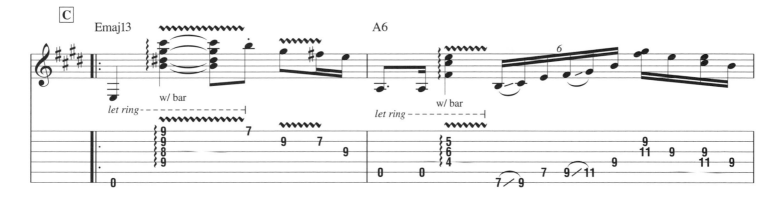

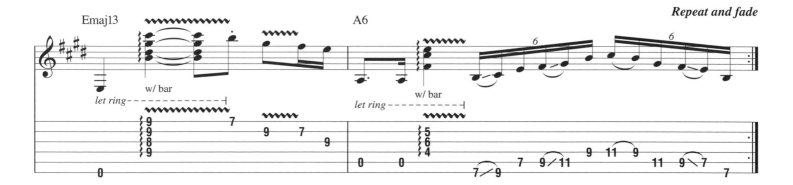

Pipeline

By Bob Spickard and Brian Carman

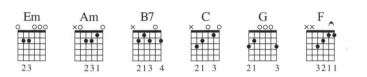

Strum Pattern: 2, 6
Pick Pattern: 2, 3

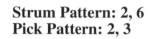

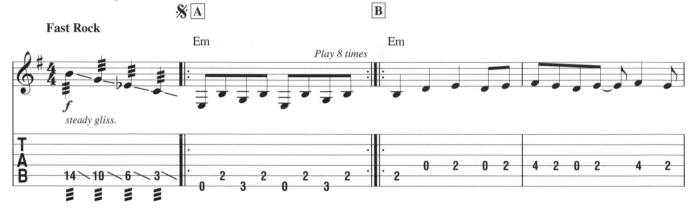

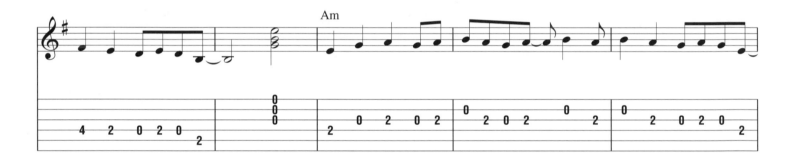

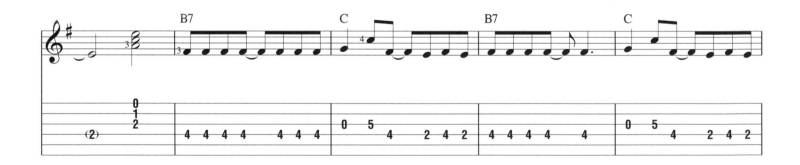

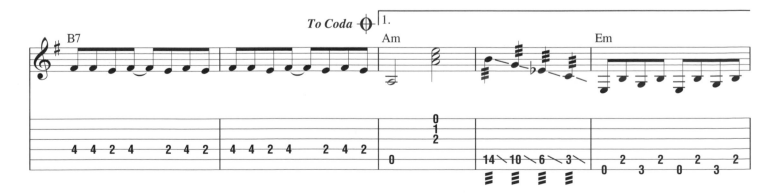

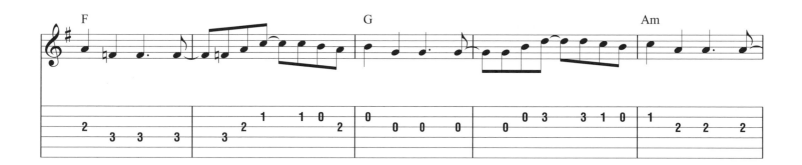

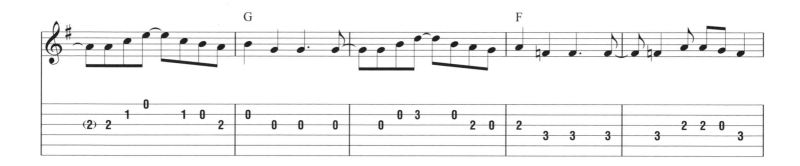

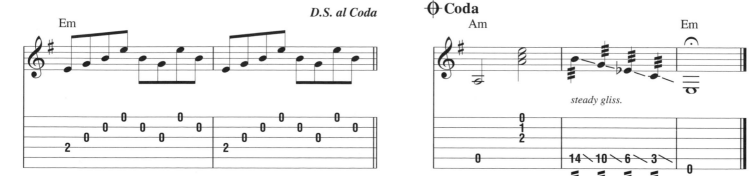

D.S. al Coda

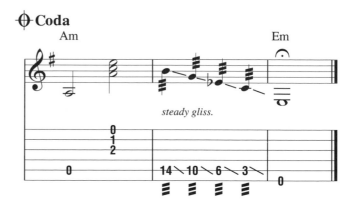

Rumble

By Link Wray and Milt Grant

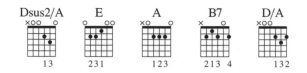

*Strum Pattern: 4

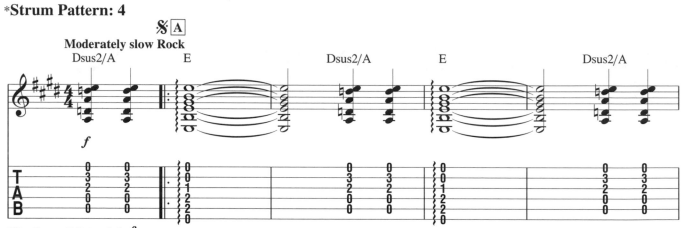

*Play Pattern 8 (2 times) for 6/4 measures.

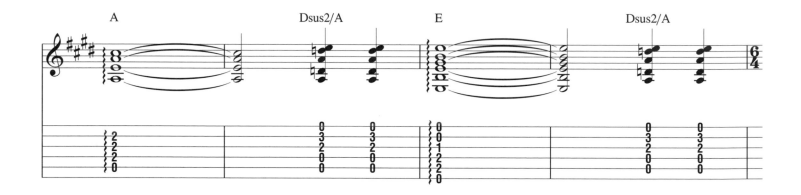

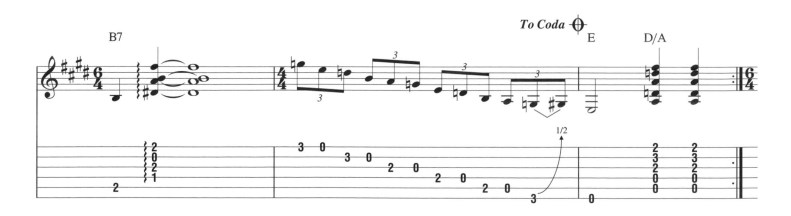

B

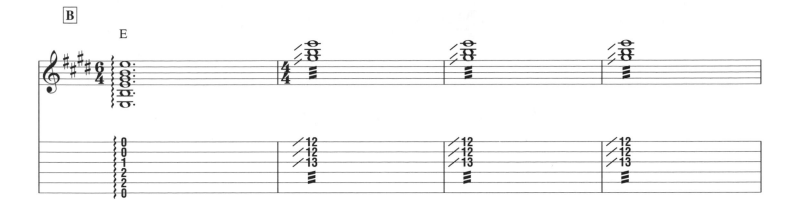

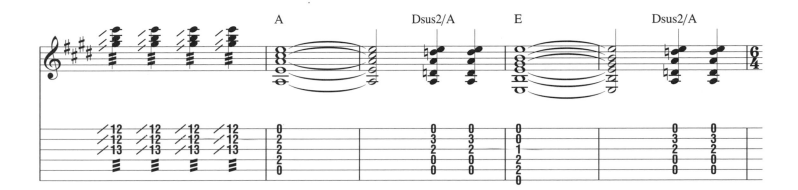

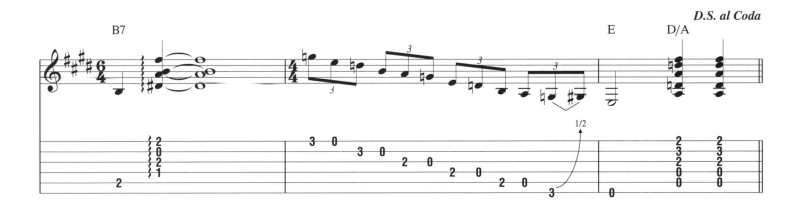

D.S. al Coda

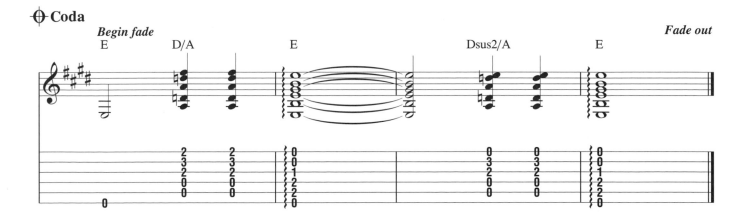

41

Sleepwalk

By Santo Farina, John Farina and Ann Farina

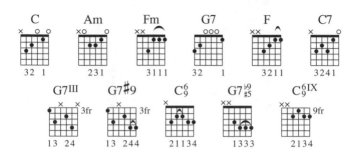

Strum Pattern: 8
Pick Pattern: 8

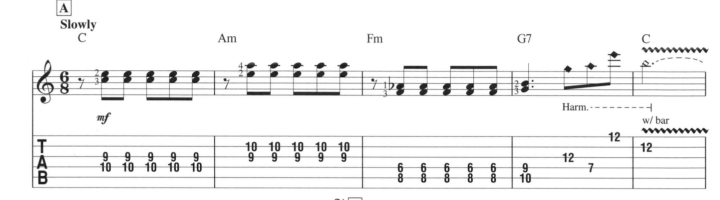

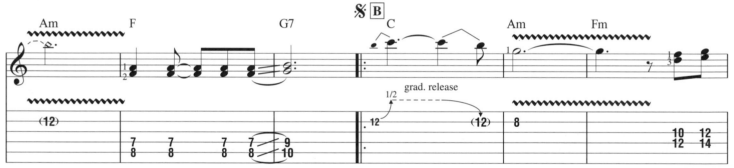

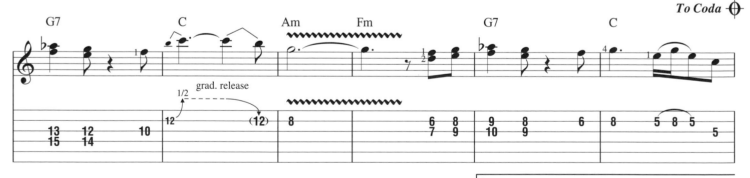

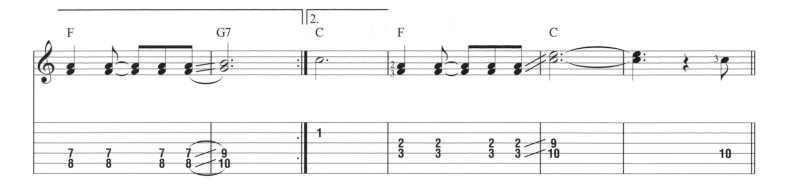

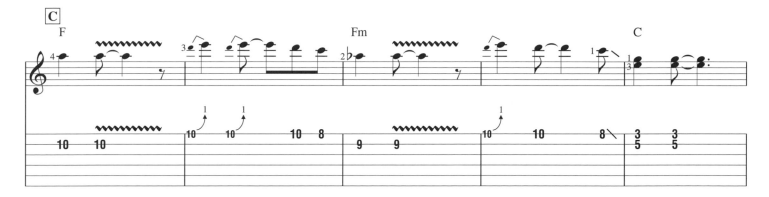

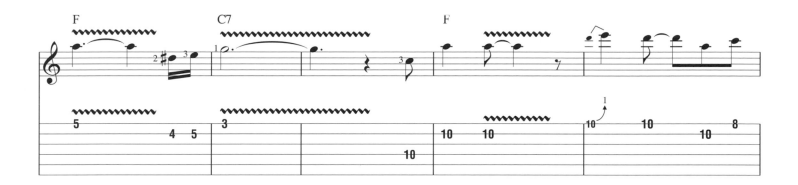

D.S. al Coda

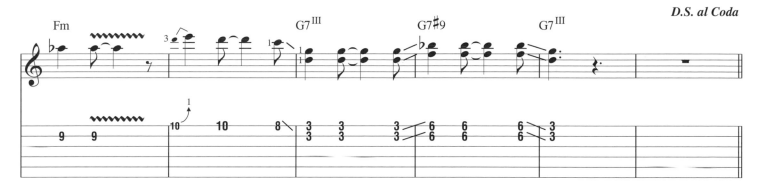

The Stumble

By Freddie King and Sonny Thompson

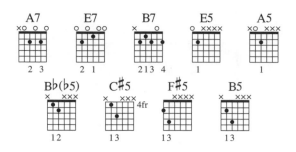

Strum Pattern: 1, 2

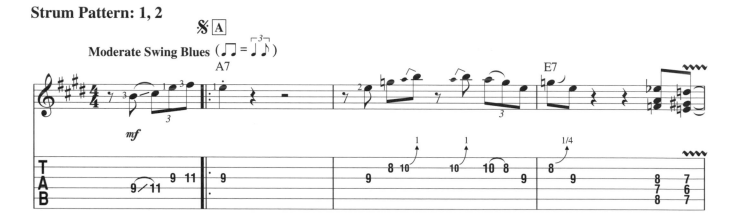

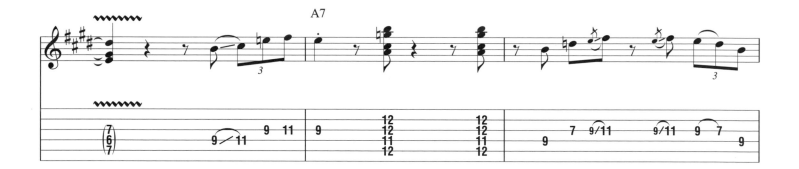

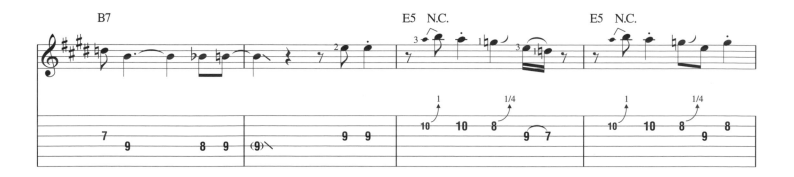

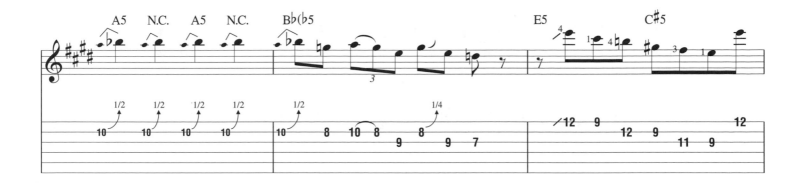

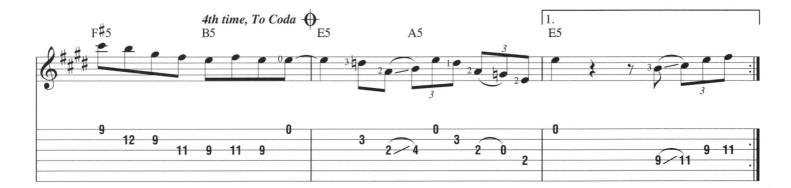

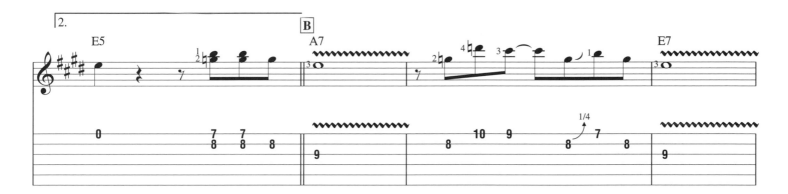

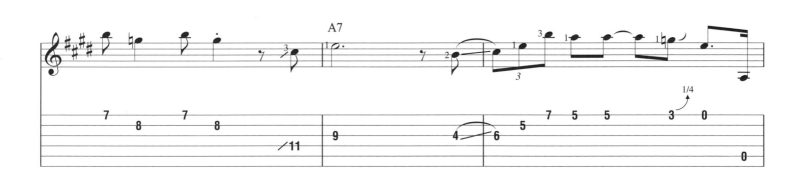

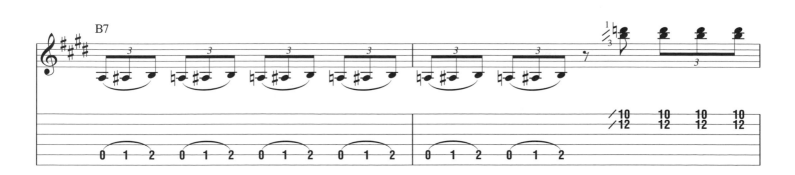

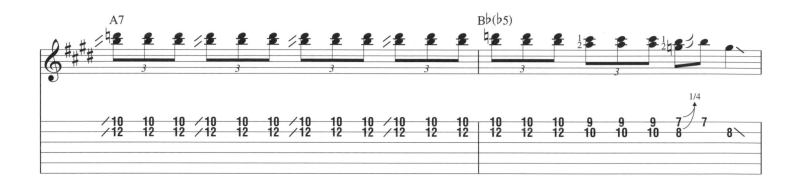

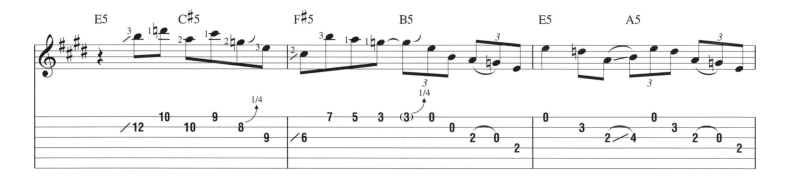

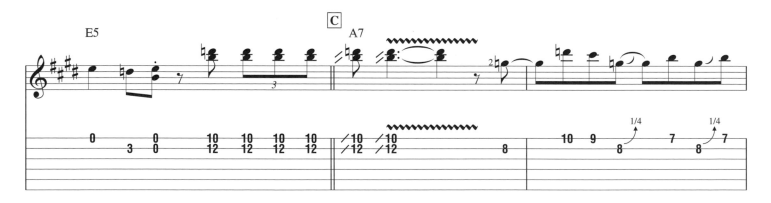

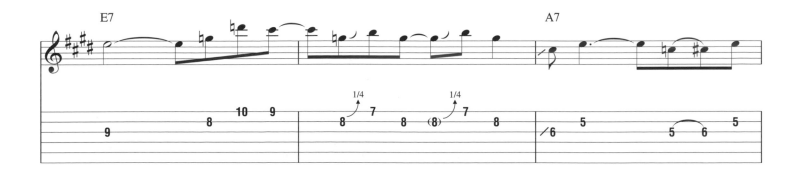

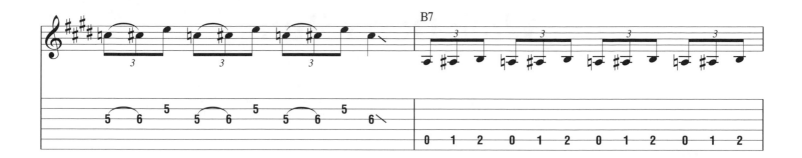

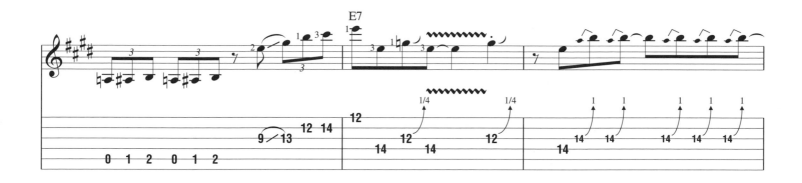

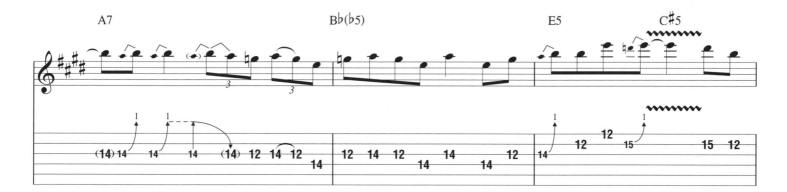

D.S. al Coda
(take 1st ending)

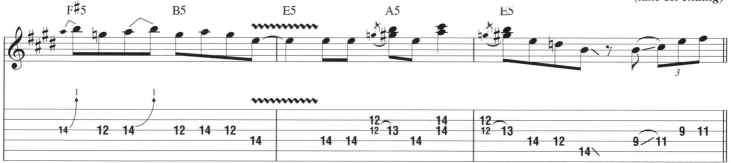

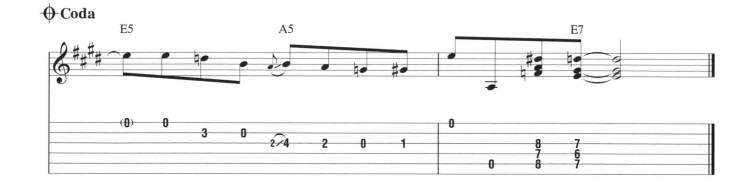

Walk Don't Run

By Johnny Smith

Strum Pattern: 1
Pick Pattern: 2

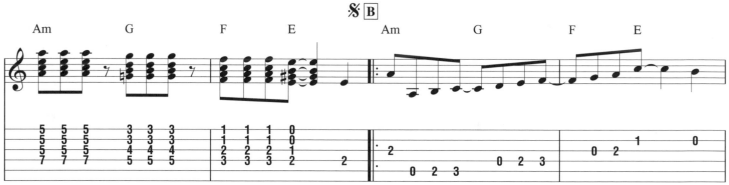

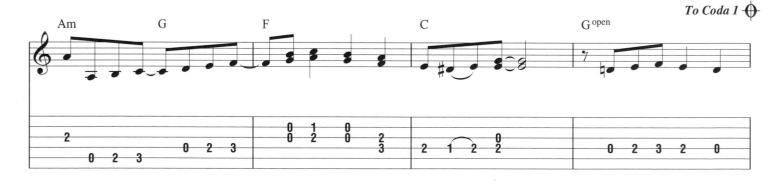

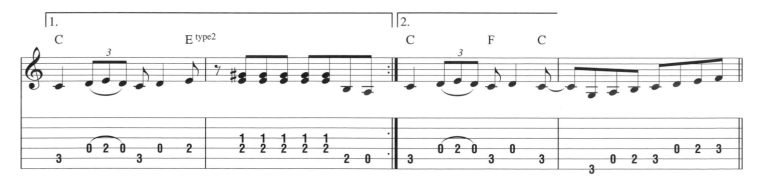

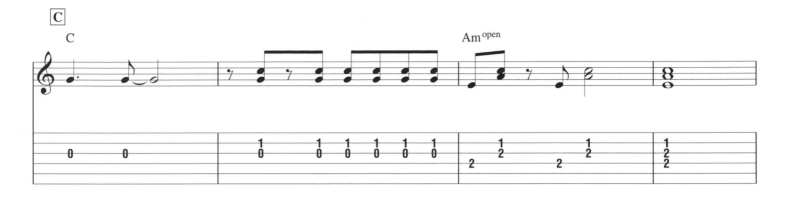

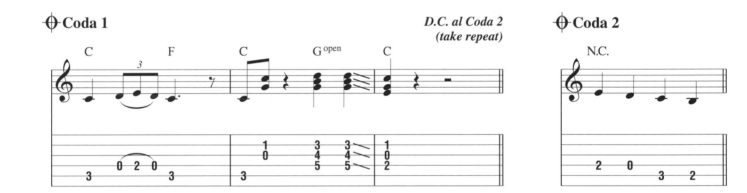

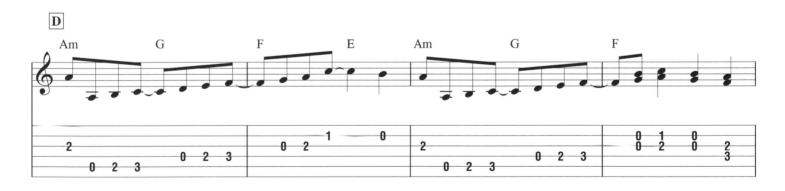

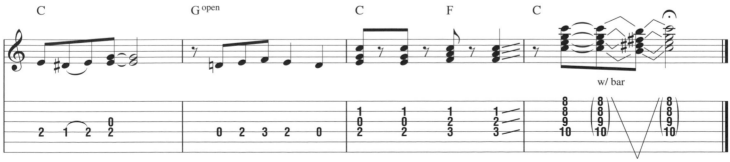

Tequila

By Chuck Rio

Strum Pattern: 3, 5
Pick Pattern: 3,4

*Use G open through E

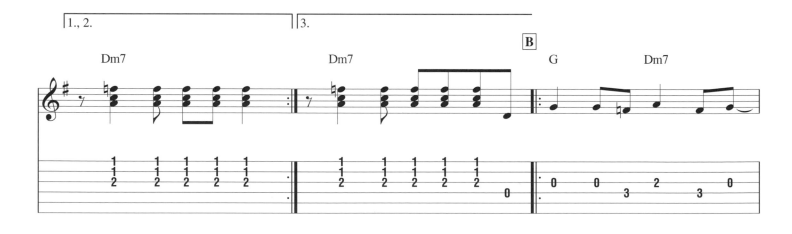

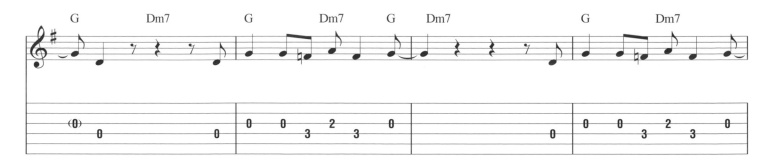

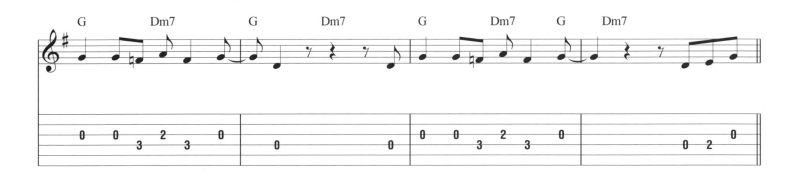

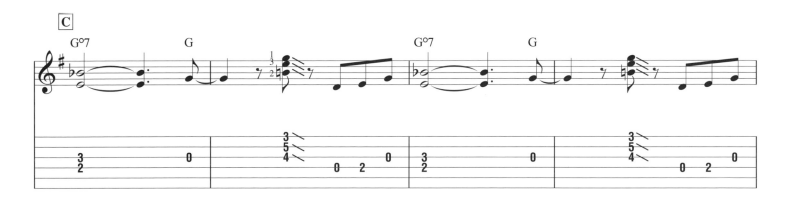

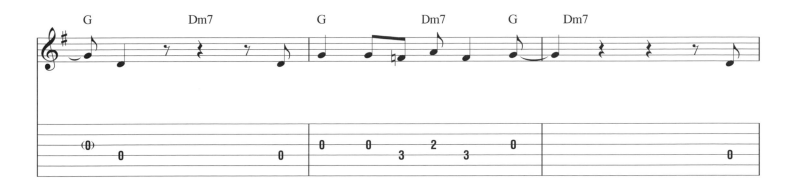

Spoken: Tequila!

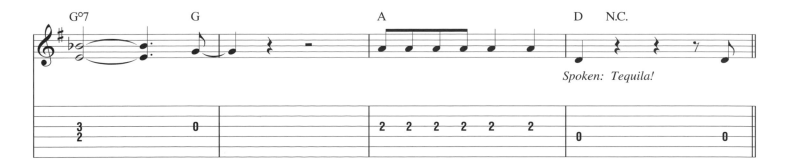

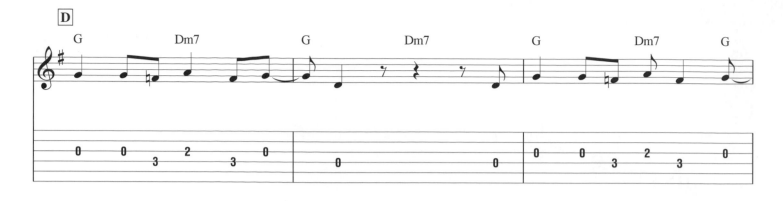

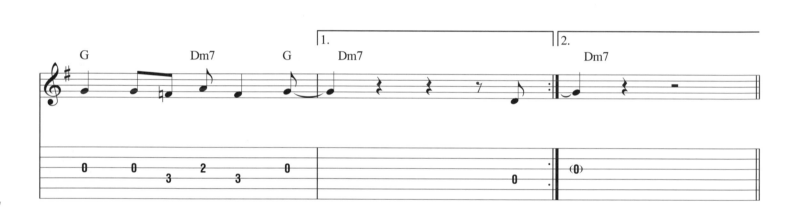

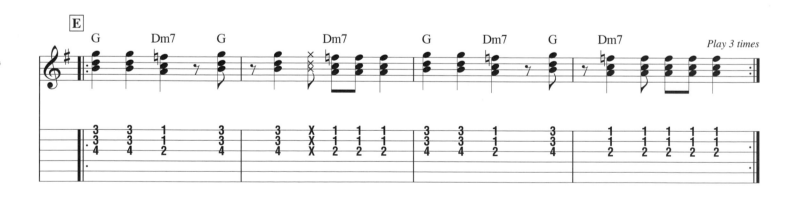

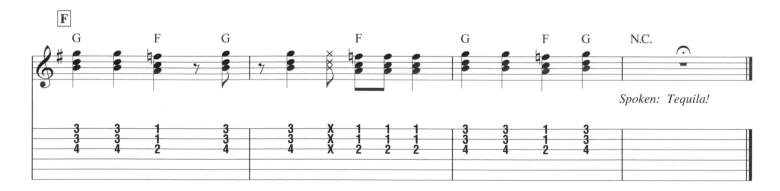

EASY GUITAR
WITH NOTES & TAB

This series features simplified arrangements with notes, TAB, chord charts, and strum and pick patterns.

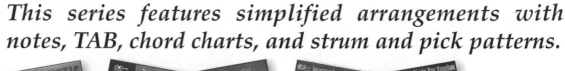

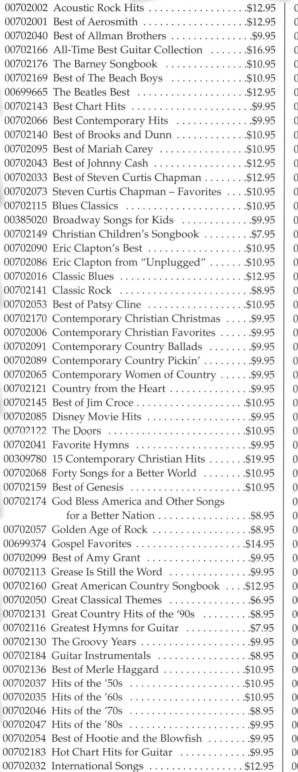

00702002	Acoustic Rock Hits	$12.95
00702001	Best of Aerosmith	$12.95
00702040	Best of Allman Brothers	$9.95
00702166	All-Time Best Guitar Collection	$16.95
00702176	The Barney Songbook	$10.95
00702169	Best of The Beach Boys	$10.95
00699665	The Beatles Best	$12.95
00702143	Best Chart Hits	$9.95
00702066	Best Contemporary Hits	$9.95
00702140	Best of Brooks and Dunn	$10.95
00702095	Best of Mariah Carey	$10.95
00702043	Best of Johnny Cash	$12.95
00702033	Best of Steven Curtis Chapman	$12.95
00702073	Steven Curtis Chapman – Favorites	$10.95
00702115	Blues Classics	$10.95
00385020	Broadway Songs for Kids	$9.95
00702149	Christian Children's Songbook	$7.95
00702090	Eric Clapton's Best	$10.95
00702086	Eric Clapton from "Unplugged"	$10.95
00702016	Classic Blues	$12.95
00702141	Classic Rock	$8.95
00702053	Best of Patsy Cline	$10.95
00702170	Contemporary Christian Christmas	$9.95
00702006	Contemporary Christian Favorites	$9.95
00702091	Contemporary Country Ballads	$9.95
00702089	Contemporary Country Pickin'	$9.95
00702065	Contemporary Women of Country	$9.95
00702121	Country from the Heart	$9.95
00702145	Best of Jim Croce	$10.95
00702085	Disney Movie Hits	$9.95
00702122	The Doors	$10.95
00702041	Favorite Hymns	$9.95
00309780	15 Contemporary Christian Hits	$19.95
00702068	Forty Songs for a Better World	$10.95
00702159	Best of Genesis	$10.95
00702174	God Bless America and Other Songs for a Better Nation	$8.95
00702057	Golden Age of Rock	$8.95
00699374	Gospel Favorites	$14.95
00702099	Best of Amy Grant	$9.95
00702113	Grease Is Still the Word	$9.95
00702160	Great American Country Songbook	$12.95
00702050	Great Classical Themes	$6.95
00702131	Great Country Hits of the '90s	$8.95
00702116	Greatest Hymns for Guitar	$7.95
00702130	The Groovy Years	$9.95
00702184	Guitar Instrumentals	$8.95
00702136	Best of Merle Haggard	$10.95
00702037	Hits of the '50s	$10.95
00702035	Hits of the '60s	$10.95
00702046	Hits of the '70s	$8.95
00702047	Hits of the '80s	$9.95
00702054	Best of Hootie and the Blowfish	$9.95
00702183	Hot Chart Hits for Guitar	$9.95
00702032	International Songs	$12.95
00702045	Jailhouse Rock, Kansas City and Other Hits by Leiber & Stoller	$8.95
00702021	Jazz Standards	$14.95

00702051	Jock Rock	$9.95
00702087	New Best of Billy Joel	$10.95
00702088	New Best of Elton John	$9.95
00702162	Jumbo Easy Guitar Songbook	$19.95
00702011	Best of Carole King	$12.95
00702112	Latin Favorites	$9.95
00702097	John Lennon – Imagine	$9.95
00699003	Lion King & Pocahontas	$9.95
00702005	Best of Andrew Lloyd Webber	$12.95
00702061	Love Songs of the '50s & '60s	$9.95
00702062	Love Songs of the '70s & '80s	$9.95
00702063	Love Songs of the '90s	$9.95
00702182	The Essential Bob Marley	$9.95
00702129	Songs of Sarah McLachlan	$12.95
00702138	Mellow Rock Hits	$10.95
00702147	Motown's Greatest Hits	$9.95
00702112	Movie Love Songs	$9.95
00702039	Movie Themes	$10.95
00702117	My Heart Will Go On & Other Top Hits	$9.95
00702096	Best of Nirvana	$14.95
00702026	'90s Rock	$12.95
00702067	The Nutcracker Suite	$5.95
00702178	100 Songs for Kids	$12.95
00702187	O Brother, Where Art Thou?	$10.95
00699261	Oasis	$14.95
00702030	Best of Roy Orbison	$12.95
00702144	The Best of Ozzy Osbourne	$12.95
00702158	Songs from Passion	$9.95
00702125	Praise and Worship for Guitar	$9.95
00702139	Elvis Country Favorites	$9.95
00702038	Elvis Presley – Songs of Inspiration	$10.95
00702004	Rockin' Elvis	$9.95
00699415	Best of Queen	$12.95
00702155	Rock Hits for Guitar	$9.95
00702128	Rockin' Down the Highway	$9.95
00702135	Rock'n'Roll Romance	$10.95
00702172	Richard Rodgers	$10.95
00702092	Best of the Rolling Stones	$10.95
00702093	Rolling Stones Collection	$17.95
00702101	17 Chart Hits	$9.95
00702137	Solid Gold Rock	$9.95
00702110	The Sound of Music	$8.95
00702010	Best of Rod Stewart	$12.95
00702150	The Best of Sting	$9.95
00702049	Best of George Strait	$10.95
00702042	Today's Christian Favorites	$8.95
00702124	Today's Christian Rock	$8.95
00702171	Top Chart Hits for Guitar	$8.95
00702007	TV Tunes for Guitar	$12.95
00309781	25 Praise & Worship Favorites	$14.95
00702108	Best of Stevie Ray Vaughan	$10.95
00702175	VH1's Greatest Songs of Rock and Roll	$19.95
00702123	Best of Hank Williams	$9.95
00702111	Stevie Wonder – Guitar Collection	$9.95
00702188	Essential ZZ Top	$10.95

FOR MORE INFORMATION, SEE YOUR LOCAL MUSIC DEALER,
OR WRITE TO:

HAL•LEONARD®
CORPORATION
7777 W. BLUEMOUND RD. P.O. BOX 13819 MILWAUKEE, WI 53213
www.halleonard.com

0203

THE BOOK SERIES
FOR EASY GUITAR

THE BEATLES BOOK

An incredible collection of 100 Beatles' favorites, including: And I Love Her • The Ballad of John and Yoko • Birthday • Eleanor Rigby • Good Day Sunshine • Here Comes the Sun • Hey Jude • I Saw Her Standing There • Michelle • Penny Lane • Revolution • Twist and Shout • Yesterday • and more.
00699266 Easy Guitar $19.95

THE BLUES BOOK

84 super blues tunes: All Blues • Baby Please Don't Go • Double Trouble • Honest I Do • I'm Your Hoochie Coochie Man • Love Struck Baby • Mean Old World • Milk Cow Blues • Pinetop's Blues • Route 66 • Statesboro Blues • Texas Flood • Trouble in Mind • Who Do You Love • more.
00702104 Easy Guitar $15.95

THE BROADWAY BOOK

93 unforgettable songs from 57 shows! Includes: Ain't Misbehavin' • Beauty and the Beast • Cabaret • Camelot • Don't Cry for Me Argentina • Edelweiss • Hello, Dolly! • I Could Write a Book • Mame • My Favorite Things • One • People • September Song • Some Enchanted Evening • Tomorrow • Try to Remember • Where or When • more.
00702015 Easy Guitar $17.95

THE CHRISTMAS CAROLS BOOK

120 traditional Christmas carols, including: Angels We Have Heard on High • Away in a Manger • Deck the Hall • The First Noel • God Rest Ye Merry, Gentlemen • The Holly and the Ivy • Jingle Bells • Joy to the World • O Holy Night • Silent Night • Still, Still, Still • The Twelve Days of Christmas • We Three Kings of Orient Are • What Child Is This? • and many more.
00702186 Easy Guitar $14.95

THE ERIC CLAPTON BOOK

83 favorites from this guitar legend, including: After Midnight • Badge • Bell Bottom Blues • Change the World • Cocaine • I Can't Stand It • I Shot the Sheriff • Lay Down Sally • Layla • Let It Rain • Pretending • Strange Brew • Tears in Heaven • White Room • Wonderful Tonight • more.
00702056 Easy Guitar $17.95

THE CLASSIC COUNTRY BOOK

101 country classics: Act Naturally • Cold, Cold Heart • Could I Have This Dance • Crazy • Daddy Sang Bass • El Paso • Folsom Prison Blues • The Gambler • Heartaches by the Number • I Fall to Pieces • King of the Road • Lucille • Mississippi Woman • Rocky Top • Sixteen Tons • Son-of-a-Preacher Man • Will the Circle Be Unbroken • more.
00702018 Easy Guitar $19.95

THE CLASSIC ROCK BOOK

89 huge hits: American Woman • Black Magic Woman • Born to Be Wild • Dust in the Wind • Fly Like an Eagle • Free Bird • Iron Man • Layla • Magic Carpet Ride • Nights in White Satin • Reelin' in the Years • Revolution • Roxanne • Sweet Home Alabama • Walk This Way • You Really Got Me • and more.
00698977 Easy Guitar $19.95

THE DISNEY SONGS BOOK

A comprehensive collection of 73 classic and contemporary Disney favorites, including: Beauty and the Beast • Can You Feel the Love Tonight • It's a Small World • Mickey Mouse March • The Siamese Cat Song • Supercalifragilistic-expialidocious • Under the Sea • A Whole New World • You'll Be in My Heart • You've Got a Friend in Me • more.
00702168 Easy Guitar $19.95

THE EARLY ROCK BOOK

Over 100 fantastic tunes from rock's early years. Includes: At the Hop • Barbara Ann • Book of Love • Do Wah Diddy Diddy • Duke of Earl • It's My Party • Jailhouse Rock • La Bamba • Oh, Pretty Woman • Peggy Sue • Rock Around the Clock • Rockin' Robin • Sea of Love • Splish Splash • Teen Angel • Tequila • The Twist • Wooly Bully • and dozens more!
00702179 Easy Guitar $14.95

THE FOLKSONGS BOOK

Over 133 classic folk songs, including: Alouette • Blow the Man Down • Danny Boy • For He's a Jolly Good Fellow • I've Been Working on the Railroad • Man of Constant Sorrow • On Top of Old Smoky • Scarborough Fair • Sometimes I Feel Like a Motherless Child • This Old Man • Wabash Cannon Ball • When the Saints Go Marching In • Yankee Doodle • more.
00702180 Easy Guitar $14.95

THE GOSPEL SONGS BOOK

A virtual bible of gospel songs. Features: Amazing Grace • Blessed Assurance • Church in the Wildwood • He Touched Me • How Great Thou Art • I Love to Tell the Story • Just a Closer Walk with Thee • The Old Rugged Cross • Rock of Ages • Shall We Gather at the River? • Sweet by and By • Turn Your Radio On • Will the Circle Be Unbroken • and more.
00702157 Easy Guitar $14.95

THE HARD ROCK BOOK

The ultimate collection of 78 hard rock must-haves, including: All Right Now • Bang a Gong (Get It On) • Crazy Train • Hot Blooded • Livin' on a Prayer • Paranoid • Rock and Roll All Nite • Rock You Like a Hurricane • School's Out • Smells like Teen Spirit • Smoke on the Water • Sweet Child O' Mine • Welcome to the Jungle • You Really Got Me • and more.
00702181 Easy Guitar $14.95

THE HYMN BOOK

An inspirational collection of 143 glorious hymns: Abide with Me • Amazing Grace • At the Cross • Be Thou My Vision • Blessed Assurance • Come, Thou Fount of Every Blessing • Fairest Lord Jesus • Holy, Holy, Holy • Just a Closer Walk with Thee • The Old Rugged Cross • Rock of Ages • more.
00702142 Easy Guitar $14.95

THE JAZZ STANDARDS BOOK

100 standard songs, including: Ain't Misbehavin' • Always • Blue Skies • Fly Me to the Moon (In Other Words) • Georgia on My Mind • I Didn't Know What Time It Was • It Don't Mean a Thing (If It Ain't Got That Swing) • The Lady Is a Tramp • Misty • My Funny Valentine • Slightly Out of Tune (Desafinado) • Stella by Starlight • The Very Thought of You • and more.
00702164 Easy Guitar $15.95

THE LATIN BOOK

102 hot Latin tunes: Amapola • Amor Prohibido • Bésame Mucho • Brazil • Cherry Pink and Apple Blossom White • Cielito Lindo • Granada • Guantanamera • It's Impossible • Mambo No. 5 • Mañana • María Elena • Perfidia • Spanish Eyes • Tango of Roses • Tico Tico • Vaya Con Dios • more.
00702151 Easy Guitar $17.95

THE LOVE SONGS BOOK

100 top love songs: Always • Body and Soul • Cheek to Cheek • Cherish • Don't Know Much • Endless Love • Feelings • Fly Me to the Moon • For All We Know • How Deep Is Your Love • La Vie En Rose • Love Me Tender • Misty • My Romance • Something • You Were Meant for Me • Your Song • more.
00702064 Easy Guitar $16.95

THE NEW COUNTRY HITS BOOK

100 hits by today's top artists! Includes: Achy Breaky Heart • Ain't Going Down ('Til the Sun Comes Up) • Blame It on Your Heart • Boot Scootin' Boogie • Chattahoochee • Down at the Twist and Shout • Friends in Low Places • Neon Moon • Somewhere in My Broken Heart • Small Town Saturday Night • T-R-O-U-B-L-E • The Whiskey Ain't Workin' • more.
00702017 Easy Guitar $19.95

THE ELVIS BOOK

100 songs from The King's career, including: All Shook Up • Are You Lonesome Tonight? • Blue Suede Shoes • Burning Love • Can't Help Falling in Love • Don't Be Cruel (To a Heart That's True) • Heartbreak Hotel • Hound Dog • It's Now or Never • Jailhouse Rock • Love Me Tender • Return to Sender • (Let Me Be Your) Teddy Bear • Viva Las Vegas • and more.
00702163 Easy Guitar $19.95

THE R&B BOOK

Easy arrangements of 89 great hits: ABC • Baby I Need Your Lovin' • Baby Love • Cloud Nine • Dancing in the Street • Easy • I Heard It Through the Grapevine • I'll Be There • I'm So Excited • Man in the Mirror • My Girl • Ooo Baby Baby • Please Mr. Postman • Sexual Healing • Stand by Me • Three Times a Lady • What's Going On • more.
0702058 Easy Guitar $16.95

THE ROCK CLASSICS BOOK

89 rock favorites: Back in the Saddle • Bennie and the Jets • Day Tripper • Evil Ways • For Your Love • Free Ride • Hey Joe • Juke Box Hero • Killer Queen • Low Rider • Oh, Pretty Woman • Pride and Joy • Ramblin' Man • Rhiannon • Smoke on the Water • Young Americans • more.
00702055 Easy Guitar $17.95

THE WEDDING SONGS BOOK

94 songs of love and devotion, including: Always • Endless Love • Grow Old with Me • I Will Be Here • Just the Way You Are • Longer • My Romance • Ode to Joy • This Very Day • Valentine • Wedding March • When You Say Nothing at All • A Whole New World • and many more!
00702167 Easy Guitar $16.95

FOR MORE INFORMATION, SEE YOUR LOCAL MUSIC DEALER, OR WRITE TO:

HAL•LEONARD® CORPORATION

7777 W. BLUEMOUND RD. P.O. BOX 13819 MILWAUKEE, WI 53213

0203

GUITAR PLAY-ALONG

INCLUDES TAB

VOLUME 1 – ROCK GUITAR
Day Tripper • Message in a Bottle • Refugee • Shattered • Sunshine of Your Love • Takin' Care of Business • Tush • Walk This Way.
00699570 Book/CD Pack......................................$12.95

VOLUME 2 – ACOUSTIC GUITAR
Angie • Behind Blue Eyes • Best of My Love • Blackbird • Dust in the Wind • Layla • Night Moves • Yesterday.
00699569 Book/CD Pack......................................$12.95

VOLUME 3 – HARD ROCK
Crazy Train • Iron Man • Living After Midnight • Rock You like a Hurricane • Round and Round • Smoke on the Water • Sweet Child O' Mine • You Really Got Me.
00699573 Book/CD Pack......................................$14.95

VOLUME 4 – POP/ROCK
Breakdown • Crazy Little Thing Called Love • Hit Me with Your Best Shot • I Want You to Want Me • Lights • R.O.C.K. in the U.S.A. (A Salute to 60's Rock) • Summer of '69 • What I like About You.
_____00699571 Book/CD Pack..........................$12.95

VOLUME 5 – MODERN ROCK
Aerials • Alive • Bother • Chop Suey! • Control • Last Resort • Take a Look Around (Theme from "M:I-2") • Wish You Were Here.
_____00699574 Book/CD Pack..........................$12.95

VOLUME 6 – '90S ROCK
Are You Gonna Go My Way • Come Out and Play • I'll Stick Around • Know Your Enemy • Man in the Box • Outshined • Smells like Teen Spirit • Under the Bridge.
_____00699572 Book/CD Pack..........................$12.95

VOLUME 7 – BLUES GUITAR
All Your Love (I Miss Loving) • Born Under a Bad Sign • Crosscut Saw • I'm Tore Down • Pride and Joy • The Sky Is Crying • Sweet Home Chicago • The Thrill Is Gone.
_____00699575 Book/CD Pack..........................$12.95

VOLUME 8 – ROCK
All Right Now • Black Magic Woman • Get Back • Hey Joe • Layla • Love Me Two Times • Won't Get Fooled Again • You Really Got Me.
_____00699585 Book/CD Pack..........................$12.95

VOLUME 9 – PUNK ROCK
All the Small Things • Fat Lip • Flavor of the Weak • Hash Pipe • I Feel So • Pretty Fly (For a White Guy) • Say It Ain't So • Self Esteem.
_____00699576 Book/CD Pack..........................$12.95

VOLUME 10 – ACOUSTIC
Have You Ever Really Loved a Woman? • Here Comes the Sun • The Magic Bus • Norwegian Wood (This Bird Has Flown) • Space Oddity • Spanish Caravan • Tangled up in Blue • Tears in Heaven.
_____00699586 Book/CD Pack..........................$12.95

VOLUME 11 – EARLY ROCK
Fun, Fun, Fun • Hound Dog • Louie, Louie • No Particular Place to Go • Oh, Pretty Woman • Rock Around the Clock • Under the Boardwalk • Wild Thing.
_____00699579 Book/CD Pack..........................$12.95

VOLUME 12 – POP/ROCK
Every Breath You Take • I Wish It Would Rain • Money for Nothing • Rebel, Rebel • Run to You • Ticket to Ride • Wonderful Tonight • You Give Love a Bad Name.
_____00699587 Book/CD Pack..........................$12.95

VOLUME 13 – FOLK ROCK
Leaving on a Jet Plane • Suite: Judy Blue Eyes • Take Me Home, Country Roads • This Land Is   Your Land • Time in a Bottle • Turn! Turn! Turn! (To Everything There Is a Season) • You've Got a Friend • You've Got to Hide Your Love Away.
_____00699581 Book/CD Pack..........................$12.95

VOLUME 14 – BLUES ROCK
Blue on Black • Crossfire • Cross Road Blues (Crossroads) • The House Is Rockin' • La Grange • Move It on Over • Roadhouse Blues • Statesboro Blues.
_____00699582 Book/CD Pack..........................$12.95

VOLUME 15 – R&B
Ain't Too Proud to Beg • Brick House • Get Ready • I Can't Help Myself (Sugar Pie, Honey Bunch) • I Got You (I Feel Good) • I Heard It Through the Grapevine • My Girl • Shining Star.
_____00699583 Book/CD Pack..........................$12.95

VOLUME 16 – JAZZ
All Blues • Black Orpheus • Bluesette • Footprints • Misty • Satin Doll • Stella by Starlight • Tenor Madness.
_____00699584 Book/CD Pack..........................$12.95

VOLUME 17 – COUNTRY
All My Rowdy Friends Are Coming over Tonight • Amie • Boot Scootin' Boogie • Chattahoochee • Folsom Prison Blues • Friends in Low Places • T-R-O-U-B-L-E • Workin' Man Blues.
_____00699588 Book/CD Pack..........................$12.95

VOLUME 18 – ACOUSTIC ROCK
About a Girl • Breaking the Girl • Drive • Iris • More Than Words • Patience • Silent Lucidity • 3 AM.
_____00699577 Book/CD Pack..........................$12.95

VOLUME 19 – SOUL
Get up (I Feel like Being) a Sex Machine • Green Onions • In the Midnight Hour • Knock on Wood • Mustang Sally • (Sittin' On) the Dock of the Bay • Soul Man • Walkin' the Dog.
_____00699578 Book/CD Pack..........................$12.95

VOLUME 20 – ROCKABILLY
Blue Suede Shoes • Bluejean Bop • Hello Mary Lou • Little Sister • Mystery Train • Rock This Town • Stray Cat Strut • That'll Be the Day.
_____00699580 Book/CD Pack..........................$12.95

Prices, contents, and availability subject to change without notice.

FOR MORE INFORMATION, SEE YOUR LOCAL MUSIC DEALER,
OR WRITE TO:

HAL•LEONARD
CORPORATION
7777 W. BLUEMOUND RD. P.O. BOX 13819 MILWAUKEE, WI 53213

Visit Hal Leonard online at www.halleonard.com

GET BETTER AT GUITAR